The science of doing better

(The 1st steps to Entrepreneurship)

Author: Isaiah Donaldson Jr.

Copyrighted © 2019 by Isaiah Donaldson Jr.

NevaEva Presents:

The Science of Doing Better

(the 1st steps to entrepreneurship)

<u>Introduction</u>

For hundreds of years we as innocent people of the world have been misguided, miseducated, and abused by a certain system.

Not being taught about a subject can have a person confused in life when it is time to respond to that subject. For instance, no one knows mathematics until it is constantly taught to them.

The brain picks up on the repetitive information being fed to it, which gives the person the ability to remember and use those formulas.

All subjects of life are taught that way. Either through the teachings of someone or upon reflecting on certain experiences.

Regardless of how a person learns a subject useful to life it still needs to be learned. Without the proper understanding of math, a person is bound not to know when, what, or how to do it.

Even though this is true, everyone gets to a point in their life in which they want to do better.

It is a natural instinct to strive for better. A lot of people want to do better than they were in the past.

For some, they may want to do better than their parents. No matter what, there is a desire in every human being to do better in life.

For most people throughout the world the concept of doing better has been used out of context.

This is ultimately because of miseducation. Just like anything else, in order to use a theory or teaching to achieve real results, one has to be taught real information!

When using false information it is almost impossible to receive true guidance from it. By not being taught correctly we as a people have slipped into a repetitive state of wrongdoing.

It is not a student's fault for being misguided by their teachers. It is their teachers fault for either attempting to hinder the students from gaining true knowledge or for attempting to teach their students about a subject they simply know nothing about!

How can a person do better when they weren't taught how?

How can a person do better when the teachers throughout their life haven't gone over this subject?

They cannot and with the wrong information installed correctly, they won't!

There is a science to everything. The only proven information that we as humans have, is science!

The purpose of my book is to educate the human mind on a scientific theory that most likely will not be duplicated in my lifetime.

"The science of doing better."

My objective is not to discredit any one's belief system, it is simply to teach the true message on a subject which we all at one time will need to learn.

Understanding how to do better and wanting to do better is completely different. I too am not perfect and was miseducated on this subject for a long time.

Until I was fortunate enough to receive true knowledge from a German philosopher.

When I first received this information it sounded so simple until I attempted it. Before I explain it to you, understand that changing does and will not happen in one second.

It takes time to go from here to there. Time is the only thing that life has no control of. You can't set a goal and expect to accomplish it without taking the proper steps to do so.

Change is a process that everyone cannot complete at the same speed, but is a process that everyone can experience. Understanding the science of doing better is the first true step to change.

Without the understanding of how to do better, how can you do better? The Webster dictionary defines the word science as "knowledge systemized and formulated with reference to general truth or general laws ."

Which basically means knowledge that can be proven.

This theory that I will speak on in this book is true knowledge which should be passed along to every loved one that you have.

The more people that you can influence to read this, the more people you can look to for help reaching the ultimate goal.

This is "**The Science Of Doing Better.**"

INDEX

Isaiah Donaldson Jr. has declared himself one of the best writers of his generation. He has been dedicated and driven for success. His ultimate goal is to help the youth develope into a great nation. A wise nation. He needs help. With the help of the people we can RE EDUCATE The Culture!!!

CHAPTER 1;

Understanding what doing better is.

Good evening, how are you doing? I see you've taken an interest in bettering yourself. That's great that you have decided to take the initial steps to do something so positive. You should be proud of yourself, but before I explain the beautiful scientific method to doing better.

Let me ask you a question or two. Why do you feel that you want to do better?

I know that you have to have a reason for wanting to do something. Is it because you're tired of being financially unstable or is it that you are tired of disappointing others?

Matter of fact to you, if you saw someone at the grocery store and they asked you what is doing better how would you respond?

Some people come up with all types of different definitions for everything. The reason why I say that is because I recently just had a discussion with two gentlemen in the Walmart plaza around the corner from Perimeter Mall located in Dunwoody Georgia.

We were speaking on what the last few presidents have done for this country. When suddenly one of the gentlemen began to explain how he wished that the people in his old Community would "just do better."

The other man interrupted him and said "well then they need to do it and stop complaining."

I noticed that the conversation began to turn into a debate because both of their views we're different from one another.

So, Kaboom! I dropped the bomb question for them both. "What is doing better?" Instantly one of the gentlemen stated, " well first of all going to better churches where the pastor isn't trying to con them."

The other guy laughed and responded, "well who cares, I don't go to church and I have a good job. They need to stop settling for minimum wage."

I listened to both of them go back and forth for almost there 10 minutes about how the people in their communities aren't trying and why they are in a bad situation.

I honestly just listened to get some insight on how other people feel about the subject.

After a while we all parted ways with both of the men huffing and puffing like they were angry with one another.

I'm not saying that I like to see two grown men argue or anything, but I'm going to be honest with you.

I did enjoy it.

Now don't talk about me because I said that. I mean of course I didn't want them to fight or anything. I just like the fact that two people that didn't know each other but still have the same enthusiasm about such a serious issue.

The only thought that kept coming in and out of my mind was. Why doesn't everyone feel this way?

How come everyone in the world doesn't feel or understand what a few people do? Why don't all people want to do better?

It's sad to say, but most of the people that I grew up with are still living the same type of life that we all hated as a kid.

For me it's different. Not to sound up in the clouds, but I'm not the same as I once was. My mind isn't the same.

My old friends probably look at me like I'm a lame or a square. I don't care. I'm proud to be a father that takes care of my responsibilities.

I'm happy that I don't have to resort to committing crimes or selling drugs to provide clothing for myself anymore, but that doesn't mean that I'm doing the best in the world.

I wish I could help everyone who is unhappy within themselves. No one should be comfortable with being uncomfortable!

The power of life is given to every living creature. In life we all have good and bad thoughts. Good and bad actions.

That doesn't mean that we are doomed for eternity. It doesn't make me a bad father because I was a bad kid!

There comes a point in time where we all have to reflect on life, but when it happens. If you are not happy with your thoughts it's time to change.

It's time to do better when you can't think about what you're doing and truly be proud of yourself. You or no one for that matter should wake up and say that you're proud of doing something that you can't stand to think about.

Everyone has to think of what they do on a <u>self conscious</u> level in order to truly understand what they need to <u>change</u>.

Think about it, why would you want to continue to do anything that you really don't approve of?

Not even what someone else doesn't agree with, but what you do. It doesn't make sense to continue any behavior that makes you mad, sad, or unhappy.

That's like me telling you that I love chicken but every time I eat it I complain because I hate the taste of it.

You would look at me like i'm crazy. That's how I look at my old friends. Now I'm not trying to belittle them, but the way that we once lived should not be okay today.

This is why I'm telling you that you don't have to continue to live in a way that you don't really approve of.

If you find yourself in life saying I want to do better, then you need to <u>think about it</u>.

I'm being real with you. Doing better starts in the mind. Why do I say that? Because there are people in different shoes that could look at someone else and make an opinion like "Oh, they ain't doing no better than nobody else."

What you do better is not determined by what someone else says, it's determined by how you feel.

If you can reflect on yourself and feel good about yourself, then that's what matters. It's a psychological adjustment that you have to make. Only you can close your eyes and dream those dreams. Only you can close your eyes and think what you think. Not anyone else.

So let's be real. When you close your eyes and think about your life, how do you feel? If you feel good about everything, then you're good, but if there are things that you think of and start to get mad, sad, or unhappy about.

Then that's what you need to change. When you have a conversation with somebody about your situation or behavior in life you should feel proud. Not uncomfortable!

If you do then that's because deep down inside yourself you wish it was different. There's nothing wrong with wanting to make things different.

There's nothing wrong with being honest about yourself, but there's something wrong with hurting yourself.

Why would you want to continue to feel or think bad about your life? You should want to be happy. Don't you want to be happy?

If so then you need to be honest with yourself. Think about what it is inside yourself or what situations that you are not happy with.

Now I'll be real. I know that sometimes that may be hard. Sometimes it's rough thinking and reminding yourself that things aren't good, but that's the first step to becoming better. How else would you know what you need to change, if you don't confirm it?

One thing about the human mind is that it will continue to remind you about your life. Your brain is the part of you that controls you.

The only way to create a more comfortable thought pattern is to "create comfortable thoughts." For most people controlling thoughts may sound easy, but for the majority of us that can be really difficult.

100% of our thoughts are not all controlled thoughts. Control thoughts or thoughts that you purposely attempt to think and direct.

If a person tells you that they have 100% control of their thoughts, they are completely out of touch with themselves.

Have you ever been doing something and out of nowhere a thought comes to you. You probably was doing one thing and Kaboom, suddenly a random thought.

Maybe about food or a TV show. You know what. How about this? Have you ever been thinking hard about an argument with someone and out of nowhere you find yourself thinking about what someone else did to you?

This is not on purpose, you might want to replay that one thing but instead your thoughts just keep jumping from one thing to another.

This itself shows that you don't have 100% control of your thoughts because if you did you would just focus on whatever it is that you want.

When attempting to do better better you have to learn how to utilize your brain. It's all in the mental.

If there is something that you're doing that bothers you. Then you have to think about what it is and how you can change it.

Only you know what you don't like or won't accept for yourself. Once you find the power within yourself to confront yourself as a Critic, then and only then, can you attempt to improve.

An emotion is just a thought. You don't know that you're unhappy until you think that you're unhappy. When a person makes up their mind and says that they want to become better. They can alter their thoughts to feel better!

It's all in your mind.

If your depressed about something like money. All you have to do is think of a way to make it better. Once you think of a way to improve the situation just stay focused on how to improve it!

If that means overtime at your job! A different job! Or borrowing it from a family member. Do what you have to do.

Now a lot of people including myself hate asking people for help, but I'll be real. That is the wrong way to be.

We all need help from time to time. No matter who you are. You're going to need help sooner or later. The sooner we give up that mentality of "oh I don't like asking people for nothing or I don't need nobody."

We can begin to improve. For real.

How many times has somebody said that they don't like asking people for help and then put them self in a worser situation.

When a person really wants to improve. They are willing to give up any bad thoughts, behaviors, and habits!

There is no way to just say I want better. It's time to grow up!

When you are mature enough to find your problem and lay them on the table. Then you know that you're ready to improve.

The Webster dictionary defines the word <u>better</u> as "to improve." So what does it mean to want to do better?

It means to want to improve. The Webster dictionary defines the word <u>change</u> as "to make different, turn, or convert."

All in all, when a person gets to the point where they think that they don't like how their life is going. It's time to improve their thoughts so that they can make different decisions!

CHAPTER 2;

Keeping Strong (Psychologically)

Okay, now that we got in a little bit out of the way let's be real with each other. Some people may not have what it takes to do better right now. That's just being real.

I'm not trying to down anyone, im just speaking the truth. Why? Because everyone is not going to be real with themselves when they read this.

I can write the best information here in this book, but there are going to be only a few people that really attempt to help themselves.

It takes a strong serious person to take real information and apply it to their life on a daily basis. Everyone just isn't strong right at this second and I can understand.

You might really know that things need to change in your life, but you're scared to lose the spouse of yours that is always pulling you down.

You might really know that you need to change your alcohol usage, but you are afraid that you won't be cool to your friends anymore.

You might really, really, really want to change you're just too damn lazy to do things different! If this is you no problem.

I'm just going to ask you to give this book to somebody that loves themselves enough or who is willing to do anything they have to do to make their life better.

Point Blank. I don't mean to sound rude, but this is serious business.

You're not going to be able to do this if you don't love yourself enough to be 100% honest.

Now I don't know you, but I know that your problems are not the same as everyone else reading this book. I'm not going to tell you that it is your fault that things aren't going the way you want them to.

I'm just not going to point the finger like that, but I will tell you that until you are true with yourself and get your situation under control. Things are not going to get better.

So it's either you're going to keep hiding from yourself or you're going to raise your head high and be strong.

We all have problems! Some small, some big. The question is when are you going to say, enough is enough?

I'm tired of being tired, aren't you? I'm tired of getting in front of people and having to feel less of myself because I know things aren't right.

You should be too. We are grown now. No one is going to stop our mind from constantly replaying our bad decisions.

It's our brain.

We have to become strong inside. The only way to overcome fear, sadness, anger, and depression is to confront the problem within yourself.

Not to throw you all off of the topic at hand, but follow me here.

I used to want to work out and get fit but I never had the ambition to go hard in the gym. I went to LA Fitness in Atlanta Georgia for the first time back in February.

I'll be real. I didn't even last 20 minutes before I was walking into the locker room ready to quit. I was all sweaty and acting like I really did something.

Suddenly here comes this big strong football player type of guy walking past me and he said "what's up little man, you gone already?For real?"

I was trying to rub it off, but it just kept replaying in my head the whole ride home. "Little man. Little man."

Thinking of how big he was. His arms were cut. He had calf muscles the size of my head. I just wanted to get right. Not too big, not too small. You know, just halfway.

I went back to the gym about a week later with my A game face on, ready to get, you know, half way big.

Man it's so crazy how it works. 20 minutes later here I am tired, walking back into the locker room. All I kept hearing was "what's up little man, you're going already? Really?"

My thoughts were eating me up because deep down I knew that I wasn't trying my best. I knew that right before I did my last set.

I thought to myself "is this all you're really going to do?" I don't know why or how. I just felt that I wasn't giving the gym my all, so I asked the guy flexing in the mirror for help.

I said, "excuse me bro. How can I get like you?" He said, "little dude you got to go hard if you want to get like the big dog, you have to set a goal that's comfortable for you and get to it. You can't get like me, if that isn't inside of you."

So I left feeling stupid because another jerk called me little. I hate when people call me little. My children's mom used to call me little, so there's this guy inside of me that hates to hear it.

But when I thought about that. I realized what the problem was. I didn't want to get halfway big for myself.

I wanted to do it to prove to her that I wasn't little anymore. I had to think about the whole picture and be true with myself. Then I came up with the plan.

I said "you know what little man it's time to get right for yourself." So I took out a sheet of paper and a pen. I wrote down my goals for my workout.

I wrote what I wanted to change about myself and why I wanted to change these things. Once I finished my list, I Googled what kind of workouts I needed to do, to get the results I needed.

I made 3 copies of the list. I put one on the front of my refrigerator. One on the middle of the steering wheel of my car and one on my office desk.

Every time I looked up I was constantly being reminded of my goals. It took me some time before it sank into my memory, but once it did I was stuck on doing better.

I started to go to the gym three days a week until I got the results that I wanted. Now I'm so happy with my body that I still go to the gym.

There's nothing wrong with being happy within yourself, I'm telling you that. The only thing that would probably make me feel better is to see that guy in the LA Fitness who told me, "what's up little man, you're going already? Really?"

I just want to show him what I was able to accomplish when I put my mind to it. You know what else? My children's mom gives me a jealous look now when she sees me.

She never thought that I would be a big dog without her, but look at me now! I've made myself proud and now I walk around with my tight shirts showing off my muscles.

A lot of people give me compliments because they remember when I was a little guy. I love it.

This feeling I get when my brain reminds me of all those things that I was called is nothing like the old feelings.

I laugh when I think about what that man said to me at the LA Fitness now. I kind of used it as motivation.

So with all of that being said, let me ask you something. Why do you want to do better?

What is your reason for wanting to improve yourself? What is your motivation?

If you are serious about doing better and I mean serious! Then I need you to get a pen and a paper. Now come on!

I don't want you to do anything that you don't want to do for yourself, but if you really want to do better than you need to take the appropriate steps to do so.

So if you're serious and you love yourself then get the paper out now. Are you ready? All right, I want you to write the title on the paper as **MY GOALS TO DO BETTER.**

You got that?

All right, now don't let me find out that you're just reading this and not going to do everything that you can't to be better. So let's continue.

I want you to write these questions, word for word.

#1) What is going on in my life that I am not happy with?

#2) Why is this happening to me?

#3) What am I doing that is allowing this to happen?

#4) What can I do to improve my situation?

#5) Why do I really want to change the situation?

Did you do it? Really?

Now for some people you may need two or more lists because you might have multiple things that you want to improve.

If that's the case feel free to do that. Whatever you need is what you need.

Do it for you, not me. Once you take your time and fill out your list completely. I want you to make copies. At least three.

I want you to think real quick. Where can you put your list that will allow you to see it constantly on a daily basis?

Wherever that place is, you need to put them somewhere that you can make sure you see it all the time so that it can sink into your <u>unconsciousness</u>.

The Webster dictionary defines the word <u>unconscious</u> as "the part of one's mental life of which is not ordinarily aware, but which is often a powerful source in influencing behavior."

This is the part of your brain that will play a big part in your downfall or success in life. If you don't know what it is or understand it. Then it can be a 50/50 chance of which one it will be, but if you can understand that your brain is the most powerful thing that you have and attempt to really use it correctly you have a big chance at "doing better."

It starts in your mind. Your goal in life should be at the front of your mind. You have to know what you want to do in order to understand what you need to do.

It's not hard to think about what's wrong in your life. All you have to do is close your eyes and let your mind drift off.

Trust me you can start thinking about anything, but if you keep thinking eventually you'll get to it. Some people are going to say "why is that?"

It's because the self conscious plays a big role in our thought process as well. The Webster dictionary defines self-conscious as "the uncomfortable consciousness of oneself."

Which simply means the inner self that is unhappy! This part of the mind is what makes people depressed or angry with themselves.

We will always know ourselves better than others, but instead of confronting ourselves as critics. We try to comfort ourselves as friends.

When attempting to do better this is a no no.

Ladies and gentlemen. Don't ever try to belittle a situation because you don't want to feel some type of way on the inside.

If it's wrong, it's wrong!

The sooner we can admit our wrongdoing the faster we can do better. A lot of people try to suppress how they feel hoping that it will make their emotions go away.

I don't know why people do this, like it's possible to hide your true feelings from yourself. It's not!

It's a scientific fact that the mine will continue to replay the memories of life until life is over.

Now I'm going to tell you a little secret. If you find yourself mad or unhappy about a situation. You will always be, until you turn that negative thought into a positive one.

That is a fact!

There are laws set by the governmental system and there are also laws given to us by what ever created us. I'm not getting religious on you, so don't get all uncomfortable and assume that I'm going to try to use this book to convert you to my religious preference.

Trust me, I'm not.

When dealing with science there are a lot of different topics, within this big topic. When it comes to us as people born in the 20th or 21st century. Most of us have been taught wrong information.

That when we hear the truth, we reject it. Now if you're a fan of my work. You already know how I do.

I love to help educate my people, so I always try to inform readers the correct way.

So here you go.

We as humans know what we know about life on Earth thanks to the people that study geology. Geology is defined by the Webster dictionary as "a science that deals with the history of the earth and its life."

There are also people that study the <u>phenomenon</u> of the universe. Phenomenon is defined by the Webster dictionary as "an outward sign of the workings of a law of nature."

Thanks to the scientific studies we know a lot about the world and how it operates. So when I speak about the universe, I'm not just making anything up to make me sound like a fool.

I'm speaking about something that most people don't know about. Why, because these things are not taught, unless you go to universities to learn it!

This is one of the reasons why I don't blame everyone for not knowing certain things. I mean how could you know when no one has talked?

There have been many great people that have tried to inform people of true knowledge throughout history, but for some reason they don't seem to get the credit that they deserve.

Like the great ancient Egyptians. They are who I give credit to for almost all of the "true knowledge" on earth. Believe it or not.

They have given the modern world so much, but that's another book in itself. The study that gave the people of today's civilization the understanding about the laws of the universe is called <u>metaphysics</u>.

The Webster dictionary defines the word metaphysics as "the philosophical Study of the ultimate called and underlying nature of things."

Now the reason why I am explaining the facts of the matter is to develop the mind of an uneducated Society.

For hundreds of years we as innocent people of the world have been misguided, miseducated, and abused by a certain system.

Not being taught a subject can have a person confused in life when it's time to respond to that subject. One certain subject that I am informing you about is "<u>the law of opposites</u>"

Which simply states that opposites attract. You may have heard that statement before, but like most things it might not have been explained to you on a need-to-know basis.

So the true meaning may have been hiding from you. This theory suggests that all opposites are meant to be together in order to balance the harmony of the universe.

For Example, males attract females, what goes up must come down, and positive attracts negative. Think about it for just one second.

Boys and girls don't have to be taught to like each other, they just do. That's how life was created, but not just for humans.

It's like that with every single living species on earth. Now of course there are a few of you wanting to dispute that proven fact with a statement about being a homosexual.

I'm not going to say anything about that but once again I will repeat myself. This theory suggests that all opposites are meant to be together in order to balance the harmony of the universe.

This is why only males and females can come together to conceive a child. Why? Because this is the way life was intended to be and continue.

Now when trying to be strong psychologically. This theory should be one to remember. Negative energy outweighs positive energy.

Negative is meant to pull and positive is meant to push. This is why people say things "like I don't need any negative people around to pull me down."

What most people don't know is that this universal law goes far deeper than that. When a person speaks they are sending energy into the atmosphere.

Which is proving to be either negative energy or positive energy. There's no such thing as in between energy.

We come from the earth, so at the time of being created. We were put here with a connection to it. This is our home and we create the environment that is around us.

We do this with the energy that we send into it. When you send negative waves into the atmosphere. They moved through the atmosphere along to come back to you.

The same as a positive energy wave would. Energy can easily be passed from one human to another. This is why a person can be feeling sad and speak to someone else about their problems and automatically make them sad.

The negative energy has passed. For example, have you ever seen someone smoking a cigarette in a room or space.

Think about how the person can blow the smoke out of their mouth and it can fill up the entire room. A person can walk right into the clouds of smoke as they enter the atmosphere.

Just like when a person passes gas. The smell seems to stay surrounding the person who passed gas and as soon as you get close enough, it just seems to hit you in the face.

This is the exact same way negative and positive energy is transferred from person to person.

When a person is happy, their positive energy can make a person feel that same way.

It's crazy, but true. This is why when people are feeling down! They need to speak with another person who might be able to cheer them up.

The only thing about this is, that the positive energy outweighs the negative energy when it is used to the same equivalency.

Which basically means positive energy waves will override negative energy waves. It's just so strong.

In order to override positive energy waves you may need about 10 times the amount of negative ones.

This is why sometimes it's hard to make someone feel better when they're sad because they may have thought so much negativity.

You have to speak so much more positively into their mind, but if you notice it doesn't take the same hard work to bring someone that is happy down.

When a person is happy you can say two or three things to them and boom. Now they're unhappy.

This is how the "law of conservation of energy" works. Now when analyzing this theory, think about what I'm about to say.

If you can attempt to use this to improve yourself, then you can become very powerful. This law means that energy can neither be created or destroyed.

It can only be transformed or transferred from one form to another. The way to use this theory for a way to do better is to utilize your positive energy.

Let's say that you're having one of those days. You're late for work because of a traffic jam.

Of course this would bring anyone's mood down. Now instead of taking your time to curse everyone out or talking bad about how your boss will be mad at you.

You should use this time to think of good things. Stay focused on your goal and don't let anything take your mind off of the prize.

Think about how this weekend is going to be or how much money you're going to make today.

Imagine your dreams coming true, so one day you won't even have to rush to get to someone else's job. Better yet, what good things can you do that would prevent you from being late to work tomorrow.

Basically I am saying. When negative things happen. Always think and speak positively.

There is no need to think negative because now you will have a negative attitude. Most negative things in your life directly point to the negative thoughts you have.

Now look at what happens when you get to work. There might be someone there that may have something to say about you being late and look at how that makes you feel.

Now you're in a worse state of mind than you were already in. Oh my God! Don't let your coworker say the wrong thing to you.

Now you're just going to have an overall bad day because of your attitude. When all it would have taken was for you to stay positive the whole ride to work.

Boom, that one little negative comment from your coworker wouldn't have even bothered you. Therefore you would continue your day on a positive note.

This is hard for a lot of people, but once again. I'm just being real. If you love yourself, then you will do whatever you need to do to make your situation better.

Always be positive within yourself. Think about who does it hurt when you're walking around thinking negatively.

Who's the one looking all mad? Who's the one making people uncomfortable? It's you!

CHAPTER 3;

The power of the tongue.

Okay now that you've thought about yourself and what you want to do, let me ask you this. Who are you going to tell?

Hold on, what? I hope you didn't just say nobody! That better not be what you just said.

Let me help you out a little bit more. When a person feels like they want to accomplish something they speak about it. No matter if it's to a friend or family member.

If a person wants to eat, what do they say to the person next to them?

"I'm hungry."

When a person has been at work all day, what do they say to the person on the phone? " I'm tired, I've been on my feet all day."

So you mean to tell me that now that you have come into realization of the power within yourself to change you're not proud enough to tell everybody that you know.

"Hey, you know something. I think that it's time for me to improve my life."

Tell your mom.

Tell your friends.

Tell yourself.

Tell your boss!

You better tell everyone that it is time for a change. This is one of your rights. Given to you by your creator.

The right to speak about your happiness. If you want anything in life you need to talk about it.

You better have not just thought, "why should I talk to people about what I'm doing?"

You should always want to speak positively about yourself. This helps you accomplish things. Think about it. If you tell someone.

"Hey I'm ready to do better."

What else can be their response except for something positive? Like "wow that's great" or "I'm proud of you."

This will make you feel better within yourself and help you stay focused. All humans deep down want to be accepted.

We all want people to acknowledge us when we are doing good. Good feedback comes with letting out good energy. You can bring something into existence when you constantly speak about it.

This is called "the law of attraction." The Law of Attraction explains that whatever is spoken or thought can be manifested.

By constantly thinking or speaking about something you are using your god-given right to create an action. This is why people say "be careful what you ask for."

This is true. You can bring a lot of great things to you if you just ask for it, but on the other hand you can also bring bad to you if you ask for it as well.

The manifestation of words is very true. For example, if a person continues to say, "I'm going to have a good day. I'm going to have a good day. There's a great chance of that person using their powers to manifest that into "true reality"

Even the guy that is always saying, " I know me and my girlfriend are going to have an argument tonight."

There's a big chance that they will. His girlfriend might not even want to but, he has spoken it into the atmosphere. He has programmed his mind to get into an argument.

He has manifested a bad attitude. So now, when he walked into the house. Shaniqua doesn't even have to say anything bad to him; he will already be on defense mode, so the littlest thing will make him respond.

Now, a big argument all because mentally he wanted to argue already!

See when thinking something constantly you are setting your mind into preparation mode. You're preparing yourself for when it happened.

This can be good, but it also can be bad. When a person speaks negatively they're just using negative energy to create their surroundings.

"I hope I don't be late for work. I hope this car in front of me doesn't stop. I hope this light won't be red for a long time. Aw man, I'm going to be late again."

Those are negative ways to use the power of the tongue. A person is really just asking to be late when they speak like that.

The universe doesn't speak English, French, Spanish, Chinese, or any other language, so it's not like the world understands your sentence in the order in which you speak it.

The world understands the energy that you put into the atmosphere! If you push positive energy out then the universe will push the same energy towards you, but if you push negative energy out the universe has no choice than to push you back with that same energy.

Think about it for real. If a person is saying all of these statements back-to-back about being late for work. Do you think that they are smiling or frowning?

Are they speaking with happiness or a little bit of anger?

Especially when the car in front of them really stops! Oh no, they might even start cursing.

Boy oh boy don't let them start cursing.

Now they are just speaking a bunch of negativity about that situation.

Guess what that does? It makes their situation worse. When speaking about anything you always want to watch your wording.

No matter how something is going, that doesn't mean that it has to continue to go that way. It can go any way you want it to.

If you need more money to pay your light bill, don't keep saying my lights are going to get cut off because if you do oh, what do you think is going to happen?

Duh, there's a big possibility that your lights are going to get cut off.

It's times like that you should be saying "what can I do to keep my lights on?"

This will tell your mind that you need it to work for you to figure out a way to keep them on! Then guess what's going to happen?

You think of ways to make it happen. You may have to ask someone or sell something.

No matter what, if you speak positively like, "I'm going to get these bills paid."

Then it will be a big chance that you will speak it into existence. This is the lowest form of the law of attraction.

I want you to understand this as the key to bettering your life!

The way to accomplish your goal is to use this law the right way. When you look deep within yourself and find something that you are unhappy with. You should reverse your feelings.

Trust me, it's easier than you think.

For instance, think about the first question I asked you to write on your "my goal to do better" list.

The question was. What is going on in my life that I am not happy with?

Let's just say the answer is, "I don't like the way my spouse talks to me."

This is a complex answer so this is why I chose it. This becomes more difficult than some because it's dealing with someone else changing.

You can't make someone else change, but you can influence them too. In this situation it is best to tell them in a very positive way <u>how you want to change your life and you would like for them to help you</u>.

Do not attack them with negative words and energy like, "you are always calling me names, you need to change because I hate it."

This will only make them defensive. You want to make them feel as though they are not the problem.

The more you speak positively to your spouse, the more positive they will speak to you.

Also, tell yourself how much better you deserve. How great of a person you are and that you know that there is someone in the world that will speak to you better.

Sometimes it's not that you need your spouse to speak to you differently. Sometimes you need a better spouse!

Say things like, " I know that I can find someone who will respect me or anyone will be happy to be in a relationship with me."

You have to speak it into existence. When you see your friends tell them how you're willing to be a good person to someone who's willing to be a good person to you.

Now I'm not saying that someone will hear you talking and walk over to you and replace your spouse. What I am saying is that by speaking like this it will prepare your mind to accept someone better.

It will prepare your mind to leave your spouse, so that you will be happy! Use your powers wisely. Don't intervene with your own success because you keep talking down on yourself.

Pull yourself up. Always!

When you get around others, speak to them positively so that they can return the positive words back to you.

Tell a stranger how you think that they look nice today so they can say "thanks, you too."

You don't have to wait for a positive energy to come to you. You can force it to come your way!

This is the biggest secret of them all! You can create your own environment by putting out what you want to come back to you.

If you want something, then get it. You don't have to wait for it to happen. You can make things happen when you think it, say it, then do it.

Now don't think I'm just talking, think about it. Haven't you heard the saying "treat others the way you want to be treated."

It's true. Whatever you want, give it. You want someone to smile at you, smile at them first. You want someone to talk to you, talk to them, don't sit back waiting for things to happen.

Take control of your life and take what you want. If you want to grow a better relationship with your mom, tell her "Mom, I love you and I want to take you out to eat."

The game of life also has its own cheat codes. There are so many people that don't understand how powerful words are.

Just like you can make a person angry or cry when you speak to them. You can make a person smile or laugh!

When you make up your mind and say "it's time to do better."

You have put the first positive energy waves into the universe. Now it's time to pile them up.

Go back to back with the thoughts. " I'm going to do better. I believe in myself. I know that I'm strong. I'm a smart person. I can do it."

Back-to-back positive thoughts. Do it. Back-to-back positive statements build a sense of confidence and happiness.

When you're happy, you're happy everywhere. Around everyone. In every situation. Don't ever find yourself saying bad things about yourself.

Think about it for real. If you can make someone cry because you have spoken to them badly.

What do you think you're doing to yourself when you speak badly about your own situations?

You should want to truly uplift yourself, not upset yourself. You're the only one that you have on the inside.

If you can't be happy within yourself, how can someone else truly make you happy?

They can't!

It starts with self. You were born you. You will die you. Therefore you will guide you. No one else! you have to love yourself.

If you love yourself, why would you talk bad about yourself? It doesn't make sense. Speaking to yourself in a good way should be your new life accomplishment.

In order to accomplish anything in life, you have to tell yourself that you want to do it. You can't want a new car, if you don't tell yourself that you want a new car!

Anything that you want to do needs to continuously go through your mind. The brain formulates ideas to achieve it. Trust me you have the power to make your life into anything you want it.

If you can think it, you can do it. You can do it!

Nothing is impossible. This is the reason why some people dream randomly and others forget their dreams.

It's your power! You have to constantly put something inside of your mind in order to create it in your life. Think of ideas that can and will help you do better.

When you do this correctly. Hold on to those ideas and make it happen. This is what is called idealism. The Webster dictionary defines the word ideas as "plans for action."

The Webster dictionary defines the word idealism as "the practice of forming ideas or living under their influence."

Now this is one of the powerful attributes of the mind. You can create an image of yourself in your mind and live by whatever that is.

It's not hard. This is what most people do anyway, they are just uneducated on this knowledge, so they don't understand that this is what they are doing.

This is why I continue to tell you that it starts in the mind because if you have the power to want better things for yourself.

Which means you have the power to speak better about yourself. Which ultimately means you have the power to do better in your life.

CHAPTER 4;

Moving on for the better.

The stimulation of the mind is a great and powerful feeling. Just to know that you are learning something new that is useful is great.

For some people they feel good in public because they know that they look good. They walk around with their heads up high because of their nice clothes, hairstyle, money, and Jewelry.

Don't hate though. It's a good feeling to know that you look nice. No one should feel bad because they take care of themselves and want to make their appearance match their feelings.

But, imagine if you could read everyone's mind when you sing them. Better yet, imagine if their clothes were their emotions.

Oh Lord! Do you know how many of those nice looking people would become bad looking? A lot of people use materialistic things like clothes and houses to attempt to define them.

If we all have the same clothes and same size houses go. How would people be identified as different? I mean if we all look alike, what would make us stand apart?

The only way to know the difference then would be to hear what a person has to say.

The personality of a person is what makes them behave the way that they do. The intellect of a person is what defines their character.

If you are wanting something different in life you have to seek something different in life.

Nothing comes to a person that can not be accepted. Nothing is in a person that a person doesn't have in them!

With that being said. When a person is ready to do better, they have to remove the bad attributes, feelings, and thoughts within themselves.

Those bad feelings and thoughts have to be replaced with good ones. This might sound hard to a lot of people. This means that you have to rethink bad thoughts in order to know what needs to be replaced.

If that's too hard for you because you have been through something that you felt was wrong, I'm going to keep it real with you.

You just gotta do it! I know that everyone's life wasn't as peaceful as others. Some of you may have been through some very bad situations.

I'm not saying that it's going to be easy to think about what was done to you or what you did to someone else. I'm just saying in order <u>to grow mentally</u> you have to be <u>true to yourself.</u>

What happened in your life that made you like this?

What was done to you that made you behave in a way that you're not proud of?

What did you do? What needs to be done in order to better yourself?

If you want better for your future, then you have to identify what and why you want to do better. Once you identify this, you need to tell yourself just like you would if you were talking to someone else.

What is it that you did wrong?

Don't sugarcoat it to make it sound as if it wasn't wrong. It was wrong. See, this next step is simply based upon the willingness to forgive and forget.

If you're not happy mentally, it's because you hold some type of feelings for someone or yourself. Maybe it's not someone. Maybe it's truly you.

No matter who did what, you have allowed yourself to fall victim to psychological guilt.

You feel guilty for either letting someone do something to you or for doing something to someone.

I'm not saying to forgive the person that did the ultimate hurt to you in the past, but I am telling you to remember that these thoughts are making you unhappy.

It might be on their mind or not. You don't know but you do know that you're still feeling some type of way. You do know that you replay everything back, wishing that you could say a few things that you didn't at the time of those incidents.

Your emotions are the reason that you can't let go. Think about it. What memories do you have that make you angry with yourself?

What memories do you have that you constantly think that if things would have gone differently, you would be better? Why don't you just forget it?

Now I know from experience what this feels like. I myself have my own problems in life.

My mother was my everything growing up. I was a mama's boy. I always wanted to hold her hand. I used to kiss her on the mouth and tell her good night until she made me stop at like the age of six.

I can remember all of the love letters that I used to write to her. All the way up until the very last one when I was 12 years old.

Everything was okay between us until she decided to move my family from New Jersey all the way to Georgia. She took me away from everyone I knew, to come to a place where I didn't know anyone. She stopped cooking dinner for me. She was never around. Man, she even kicked me out.

At the time, to me she turned into a bad mom fast. That's how it seemed to me, so that's how I say it. I hated this new mom that I had.

I just wished that she would have stayed the same. I used to replay a lot of bad times that we had together in my mind. There were a lot of things that I wouldn't say to her at those times.

So, do you know what I used to do? I used to yell at her in my mind and change the whole conversation around. For real. Everything that I imagined myself saying to her that I didn't really say in real life.

I imagined certain situations that had occurred in the past. Before I knew it, me and my mother would be having a whole new argument, that truly never even happened.

For a long time in my life until I spoke with a counselor about a few things. I didn't know who else to talk to. My counselor made me realize all of those things.

I made up arguments in my mind with my mom. In reality, hat was only me arguing with myself! So, I'm going to ask you.

Has this ever happened to you? How often do you find yourself replaying old situations where you switched some of the words around to say what you think you should have said before?

Who were you arguing with?

Now, of course you might be thinking that you were arguing with your mom, sister, father, ex-spouse, or whoever that person is.

I'm going to keep it real with you like I have been. You weren't! You were arguing by yourself, with yourself.

Think about it. Who was thinking those thoughts? You. Who was the one going back and forth? You!

So basically you were arguing with yourself. No wonder you get mad every time you think of this person. Every time you do, they always have something new to say to you!

They're always saying bad things, huh. No, it's all just in your mind. You're turning real problems that you have had in life into <u>notional</u> ones.

The Webster dictionary defines the word notional as "existing in the mind / unreal."

So, what you are doing my friend is using your own thoughts to hurt yourself. This is why it seems hard to move on because you're trying to hold onto their actual statements and your own hurtful words.

This is common for people to do. People tend to hold themselves hostage psychologically. They trap themselves with negative energy and make it hard for it to go anywhere.

Why, though? Why do you want to prevent yourself from achieving happiness? Why do you yell at yourself at night?

What happened? I need for you to figure it out because in order for you to improve psychologically you have to let go of the pain and bitterness.

Hurting your own feelings and emotions in your own brain only hurts you! Think about it now, please! Play those awful thoughts now, but instead of yelling and screaming like you used to. Say I apologize.

Tell that person that hurt you. I forgive you for hurting me. I'm not mad at you anymore. I'm going to move on in life.

This may be hard, but trust me it works. Anytime from here on out when you think of these bad, tragic situations remember that it's over now.

It's not ever going to happen again, unless you make it happen in your mind. Stop living in the past!

I know it's easier said than done. I know how long it took for me to get over all of those things that happened between my mother and I. But guess what?

I did. Now I feel better deep within myself. I'm not hurting and neither should you. It starts in the mind! Do you really want to do better?

Do you?

Well then tell yourself to smile throughout the day. Allow yourself to smile throughout the day. Don't continue to shield yourself. Enjoy your life.

Forgive and move on! It's not about no one else but yourself. You should be tired of letting your own thoughts make you mad.

You should be able to make yourself happy. No one loves you like you love yourself. This is true and don't ever forget it.

You out of all people should want your show to be happy. You shouldn't be making yourself cry. Don't you love yourself?

How about you say it? "I love myself. I want to be happy and I'll do whatever it takes. I will do better, no matter what. I will forgive and move forward!"

CHAPTER 5;

Improving in life.

Fixing, fixing, fixing. If your life is broken, come get a fixing. It's time to go out tonight for some fun. Whose all going?

It is summertime and your favorite Rapper is coming to town. Let's go have a ball, who's coming? I think we should rent the limo. What do you think, we ain't living life?

We're going to have a great time tonight. Who's coming? Everyone needs to chip in $400. Oh what, you ain't got no money to have fun with me? Why not? Do you have a job?

Haha! I'm just joking everyone. But, what if I was serious? If I was your friend and I told you all of that, what would be your response?

Would you be able to go? I'm talking about the best event of the summer. I know a few of you are saying "oh yeah I would go," could you afford to ball out with me.

I remember a few times when I couldn't go out and enjoy myself with my friends. They would always tell me later on how much fun they had and what celebrities they saw.

No lie. It used to piss me off. I'm going to be real with you. I'm not a hater or anything, but why are they always able to have so much fun?

They were out having fun and here I was. The boring little duckling that can't never afford to do anything. I used to hate it.

It was so bad that I had to make some adjustments. I wasn't going to keep being looked at by my own friends like the broken mirror.

How many of you feel like the broken mirror? How does it feel knowing that there is so much to do and you can't do any of it?

Now let's be honest, why can't you? For real. Why can't you enjoy your life to the fullest? Is it because you don't have the money, are your children stopping you, is your spouse boring?

Whatever it is, it needs to change. Fun comes with life. For most people fun is a stress reliever. Laughing is great, so why are you depriving yourself?

I don't want to hear, "man I'm too old for that." There are always fun things to do. For people of all ages. Some of you aren't happy with life!

This is why you're always looking on social media, trying to see what everyone else did over there weekend. I have small children, so I can understand a single parent thinking that they can't leave their children at home alone.

That would be child neglect and in no way would I condone that. For all of you that are parents. How about you weigh your options.

Maybe the grandparents or babysitter can keep them while you go have a nice outing. If you can't do that, then what about taking the kids with you.

No, no, no. Not to the club! Maybe to Six Flags for some fun family time though. Trust me, if you need to have some fun then so does your family.

A lot of people work Monday through Friday and just sit at home on the weekends. I do but then again I don't! I like to go out and mingle with people.

I always like to watch my children have fun and there's nothing wrong with that. For parents like me! I suggest that you find other parents that are similar.

Take your children to family events and mingle with other parents. Start to become friends with people that have children, your children's age.

Now watch the fun come along. Get to know a few people, so when your children want to step out and go to a friend's house, you can too.

Stop being so boring! You only have one chance to live this life and you better enjoy it. What about you? You know, you! The one reading this book that is financially struggling.

Don't you want to have fun? Not even a little, huh? So, you just want to mope around the house and let life pass you by. well not anymore.

It's time for you to do better. You're old enough to know why your life is the way that it is. Don't stress yourself out by sitting in the house all weekend thinking about it. Get out and live. You don't need a million dollars to enjoy yourself.

There are so many free things going on this weekend. Stop belittling your situation by saying "I ain't got no money for that stuff, I got bills."

The park is free. You don't like free things either, huh? Well I'll tell you what. How about looking on Google. Google knows everything, trust me.

Look on Google for fun things to do near you and see what's in your price range. Trust me, fun is a must in life.

You need to enjoy life, but the financial part is a whole nother book in itself. If you need guidance on the financial fundamentals of life, I wrote another book that you need to read after this.

It's called why we're broke and very rich. It's a great insight to most of the world's financial problems.

I want you to stay focused right now and remember what the objective here is. Doing better! Let's not focus on money, unless that's your problem.

Let's not focus on the children stopping you. Let's focus on you. Why do you feel as if you aren't enjoying your life to the fullest?

What are some things that interest you? If you don't mind. Grab that pen and paper of yours. Now don't try to be all funny now. Get the pen and paper.

This is for you ladies and gentleman, not me. I want you to title the paper. "What's up!" I don't mind if you laughed at my title go ahead, but make sure you do it.

All right? Now the purpose of what's up is to find out some things about yourself that you don't think about on a daily basis.

So, please take this seriously because I promise you that it will help you start enjoying life a little more.

I want you to write a 7 sentence summary of what you think you missed out on as a kid.

Also I want you to answer these questions.

#1) What do I feel like I got deprived of growing up?

#2) What did I always enjoy doing as a kid?

#3) Where were my favorite places to eat growing up?

#4) If I was rich at 10 years old what would I have done for fun?

Now when you're finished writing down these questions. Really take your time to think about the answer.

The purpose of these questions is for you to tap into the inner you. In order to enjoy your life. You should take in consideration what life was like when you stopped enjoying it!

Why did you stop enjoying your life? A lot of people, including myself, weren't in a position to have fun as a child though.

If your parents were poor, always busy, or if you had no friends. You still wanted To have fun, but not enjoying your childhood turned into an unhappy adulthood.

Feelings of unhappiness don't go away because a person turns a different age. Age has nothing to do with the emotional progress of a person.

Emotional change some times depends on the environment. When a person is stuck in one situation, their mood tends to stay the same.

Whatever a person wants and likes at the age of 12. They most likely will like and want at 13. The only way things change is if something changes their perception of it.

So, what changed your perception of fun? What made you not interested in enjoying your life anymore? If you say that nothing happened, then why aren't you enjoying it?

What can you accomplish that will make you say hey I'm happy. This should be your ultimate goal. To be happy in life. This should be one of your only goals.

CHAPTER 6;

Improve your connections.

How many of you are connected with people doing what you want to do? I might be moving a little too fast. Let's start over.

Friendships and families play a key role in everyone's life. Most people spend the majority of their time at work.

More time at work than with our loved ones. Very few of us enjoy being alone all of the time, but how many of you have friends and family members that just aren't doing what you need them to be doing?

You know the person that you talk to all the time, that always makes you think. "You ain't never doing nothing."

How about. "You ain't never got nothing positive to say." This is most of us. Why do we sometimes accompany ourselves with people that just aren't doing anything?

In order to change your life, you have to re-evaluate your situation because your environment plays a key role in your life.

Have you ever heard the saying you are a product of your environment? It's true. Most of the people that are not doing what they want to do in life are surrounded with people that aren't doing what they want to do in life as well.

You are a reflection of the company you keep. Unhappy people live and work around unhappy people. This is why they tend to stay unhappy because they have no one around them that can help their situation.

When people find themselves around others that they don't have anything in common with they don't befriend them! They get away from them!

Think about it. Rich people normally have rich friends. Poor people normally have poor friends and cool people always have cool people. Meanwhile the Nerds were always together.

This is how the world works. You don't see cats playing with dogs. You see cats playing with cats. Dogs playing with dogs. If you look at your friend like you don't belong with them, then why are you with them?

Friendships play a big role in a person's unhappiness, like how can you be happy when you're broke and bored! Then you call all of your friends and they're broke and bored!

Friendships can influence a person to do better or worse. If you have friends that are always thinking negatively, how can they influence you to be positive?

All they can do is be themselves. If you want to do better, you have to have better friends! If you are smart and all of your friends are not. What can they teach you?

What can you learn from someone who can't teach you? How can you do better when no one you talk to is doing better? You need friends that can either help you realize your potential or help you reach your potential.

All in all, you need friends that can help you. If you want to be rich, how is being around poor people going to help you?

If you want to learn how to play football, how is joining a basketball team going to help?

You need to be around people that are doing the kind of things that you want to do. I'm sorry if that makes you rethink your relationship, but you actually might have to.

How are any of your friends helping you be who you want to be? If you can think of people that are helping your life then that's good.

I'm not saying be fake. I'm not saying blame everyone else for your problems. What I am saying is if you have someone close to you who is not helping you do better, they are helping you be worse!

When a person reaches their breaking point and says it's time to do better, they need to evaluate everything! Past, future, self, and environment.

Think about it. If you want to go have a good time at the Drake concert then this is what you want to do! You go to your friend's house and say "hey let's go out for drinks."

Your friend responds, "sorry I can't go because I don't have any money." Then you go to your other friend's house and say "hey let's go to the Drake concert on Friday." This friend says, "sorry I would love to, but I don't have the money."

Then you go to your other friend's house and say, "hey let's go to the Drake concert on Friday. It starts at 8 and it's going to be so much fun." Then they say, "oh man I would but I don't have a babysitter."

Now that you don't have anyone to go with you don't even go but that's what you wanted to do! So in this aspect your friendships hindered you from enjoying your Friday night.

So you end up sitting in the house bored scrolling up and down your Instagram watching everybody else post pictures at the Drake concert.

Now don't be unhappy because everyone else is enjoying themselves. What you need to do is find new friends or just start going out alone!

If you don't talk to anyone that is able to do it with you, go do it alone! Trust me. There are a lot of people that go and enjoy things alone.

You can actually find a lot of good connections that way. Step out of your small box and get into the mix. Don't be afraid to mingle with people that you don't know.

That could be the start of a great relationship. There are tons of people that are attempting to do better in life that may not have anyone close to them that are willing to take those same steps.

Guess what they did? They decided to go out alone and enjoy themselves. There is nothing wrong with going out by yourself.

That is also a great way to get in touch with the inner you. Go out and take a deep breath. Take some time to be alone and get away or to get to know some new people.

There is nothing wrong with having new friends. Especially when your old friends are not doing what you need them to do for you.

Don't hold yourself back from being great because you don't want to leave some people behind. I'm not trying to sound like a bad guy or anything.

I'm just being honest. With time comes change. People change as they get older. Now, if you find yourself wanting to get better. Then you have to acknowledge your true feelings.

Don't ignore how you feel because it means that you might have to let go of a few things from the past. This is how life goes.

We as people sometimes get tired of being a certain type of way, which makes us get tired of certain situations. This is good.

You want to reach this point in life. It's not a bad thing. There is nothing wrong with wanting to do better, but there is something wrong with wanting to do worse!

When you reach a point of wanting to do better for yourself. There should be nothing stopping you from achieving what you want.

So once again let me ask. How many of you are connected with people doing what you want to do?

CHAPTER7;

The power of improvement.

Now that we have reached the Final Chapter. I want to let you know something. Feeling proud of oneself has to be one of the best feelings that is not spoken about.

Self-awareness. This is the power of the mind. Your mind is strong and powerful. You can literally become anything you think of!

It's all up to you. Do you want to be happy? Then think happy thoughts! It starts in the mind!

Before your arms can turn the steering wheel of a car and prevent you from getting into a car accident. Your mind has to tell your arm to do so.

Ultimately your mind and thoughts control all of your actions. So therefore, if you can think it, you can do it. If you want something to happen for you. You first have to think of what you want.

Then you have to think about how it can happen. Next, you have to think about what you have to do to make it happen. You have to make it happen though!

Just the thought of wanting something will make you happy. You only become unhappy when you think you cannot do it! There is no truth until it is proven.

Which means nothing is done until it is done. Nothing is unaccomplishable until the mind thinks that it cannot be done! Self-awareness can reflect inner happiness or inner sadness.

It's only based upon what is inside. Whatever lives within, will be within. Until the inner self is happy, it will be sad!

No one should stop themselves from reaching true happiness, but most of us do. It's not on purpose. This is mainly due to mis-education and misunderstanding of self.

Know thyself is a saying which means so much more than what has been explained.

We all we're giving some type of strength. All of the things that were given to us at birth should be taken advantage of before death!

There's no stopping the mind from thinking until the mind stops working. Therefore our actions and experiences will continue to be trapped in the mind.

There's no reason for you to trap bad things inside. Bad feelings and bad thoughts should be replaced with good ones.

Sadness should be replaced with happiness. No one should settle for anything less than what they want to. So, if you picked up this book with thoughts in your mind about changing. That is what you should be attempting to do everyday.

Life is not just a one-day process. Neither is change. It takes individual days from birth to death. Which means change doesn't just happen overnight.

It is a process that may take a lifetime. It may take months. No one can put a time frame on the ability to develop better habits and thoughts.

No matter how long it takes though. It should be taken seriously. All of the elements of change should be what you mean. Not just one thing will make a person reach their full potential but all useful lessons. This is the science of doing better. The first step to entrepreneurship.

Facebook: Neva Eva

Instagram: NevaEvaRecords

About the author;

Hello, I am Isaiah Donaldson Jr the author of this wonderful book.

I am from Newark New Jersey and at this moment in time of actually writing this book I am 27 years old.

I have two beautiful children Amir and Isabella.

I've been through a lot at this time.

I've been incarcerated.

I am not proud to say it, but I am definitely happy to have learned from each and every one of my mistakes.

We as humans do make mistakes and that's one thing that people have to realize.

It is common to make mistakes.

I've been in relationship after relationship after relationship.

So I definitely know a little bit about them.

I'm a great father and for some that may be hard to believe being in the store I'm young and I am African American.

I took my time writing each and every one of my books in the different phases that I was in at the time of writing them.

I never wanted to go on to my next course in life without writing down my previous one.

So after a horrible relationship with my children's mom.

I decided to write this book to inform my future girlfriend how to keep me!

Just because I am from a bad place and have been incarcerated does not mean that I don't deserve to be loved.

It does not mean that I don't know how to treat men.

 It does not mean that I am a deadly father.

My past is my past and my future is my future.

 I will not use my past as an excuse for my future. I will use it as a learning tool in order to correct my present, and manifest my future.

Other books by Isaiah Donaldson Jr

- How to raise boy to be a man
- Why we're broke and they're rich
- How to turn a boyfriend into a husband
- Why boys join gangs

Made in the USA
Columbia, SC
04 September 2022

65984635R00052